A 3-minute forever book

EAT YOUR PEAS®

for New Moms

By Cheryl Karpen
Gently Spoken

To _____

With love from
_____

Congratulations!

Life
as you know it
is about to **change** forever.

And for the better!

Will it be easy?
Not on your life.

But it will be
wonderful.
Exhilarating.   Exhausting.
Sometimes scary.
And always
Surprising.
Which brings me to the reason
for this little book.

With all this **newness** in your life,
you are not alone.
I promise.

Want to talk?
Here's my number
(in case fatigue affects your memory)

_____

Call me!

If you ever want to
brag a little
(or a lot),
if you ever need a good **laugh**,
a good **cry**,
or just some good old adult
conversation

Call me.

I promise to listen
(really listen)
with all my heart.

What's more, I promise I won't get
carried away with free advice
(unless, of course, you really,
really want some!)

In the meantime,
here's a little homegrown wisdom
to go with the wonder of your

new little sweet pea...

May your days
be filled with
hugs and
giggles
and
silly things
only a mother could love.

When the baby keeps you
awake all night,
remember you will have
a lifetime to catch
up on your sleep.

But you'll never
have this night
with your **little one** again.

There is nothing quite as sweet as baby toes.

Kiss them often!

What you didn't
get right today
you can practice again
tomorrow.

(After all, isn't that what
you will teach
your Little One?)

Keep a **calendar** handy
to jot down those
precious things
your baby does.

Years from now,
you'll be glad you did!
(And so will your baby.)

Be patient with yourself.

This is definitely
on-the-job training.

Go with the flow

will come to have many
new meanings.

Enjoy them all!

Whatever you
dream
for your baby,
be sure to keep dreaming
for yourself.

You will be richer for it.

There is no such thing as a perfect mom!

Give yourself the same compassion and understanding you would give to others.

Record your
B A B Y's
laughter.

It's a sound worth saving
forever.

Begin cultivating babysitters now. At the first sign of cabin fever, call one!

You can never take too many pictures.

Make sure you are in some of them too!

And remember to stay healthy,

Eat Your Peas!

photo
of
your sweet pea

Why Peas?

She was a vibrant, dazzling young woman with a promising future.
Yet, at sixteen, her world felt sad and hopeless.

I was living over 1800 miles away and wanted to let this very special young person in my life know I would be there for her across the miles and through the darkness. I wanted her to know she could call me any time, at any hour, and I would be there for her. And I wanted to give her a piece of my heart she could take with her anywhere—a reminder she was loved.

Really loved.

Her name is Maddy and she was the inspiration for my first PEAS book, **Eat Your Peas for Young Adults**. At the very beginning of her book I made a place to write in my phone number so she knew I was serious about being available. And right beside the phone number I put my promise to listen—really listen—whenever that call came.

Soon after the book was published, people began to ask me if I had the same promise and affirmation for adults. I realized it isn't just young people who need to be reminded how truly special they are. **We all do.**

Today Maddy is thriving and giving hope to others in her life.
If someone has given you this book, it means **you are pretty special** to them and they wanted to let you know. Take it to heart.

Believe it, and remind yourself often.

Wishing you peas and plenty of joy,

Cheryl Karpen

P.S. My mama always said, "Eat Your Peas. They're good for you!"
The pages of this book are filled with nutrients for the heart.
They're simply good for you, too!

The newest little sweet pea in the
Eat Your Peas Collection
was lovingly made possible by Team Peas.

My heart is grateful to:

Editor, Suzanne Foust
for lending her creative voice and new mom wisdom.
You are all heart and it shows!

Illustrator, Sandy Fougner
who spent sleepless nights birthing new designs
and pouring love into each page.
You are truly a gifted artist!

A special thank you to
Eat Your Peas readers and receivers
who are *our* true inspiration. Thank you for believing in the
power of PEAS to inspire, uplift, and encourage.

You are cherished.

 **Cheryl**

About the author "Eat Your Peas"

A self-proclaimed dreamer, Cheryl
spends her time imagining and creating
between the historic river town of Anoka, Minnesota
and the seaside village of Islamorada, Florida.

An effervescent speaker, Cheryl brings inspiration,
insight, and humor to corporations,
professional organizations and churches.
Learn more about her at www.cherylkarpen.com

About the illustrator

Sandy Fougner artfully weaves
a love for design, illustration and
interiors with being a wife
and mother of three sons.

Other books by Cheryl Karpen

The Eat Your Peas Collection™

is now available in the following titles:

Tough Times	Daughters
Someone Special	Sons
Me	Sisters
Teachers	Mothers
Teens	Fathers
Holidays	Grandkids
Daughter-in-law	Grandparents
Mother-in-law	Sweethearts
Sister-in-law	Girlfriends
For the Cure	Birthdays

New titles are SPROUTING up all the time!

Heart and Soul Collection

To Let You Know I Care
Hope for a Hurting Heart
Can We Try Again? Finding a way back to love

To view a complete collection, visit us online at www.eatyourpeas.com

Eat Your Peas® for New Moms

Copyright 2005, Cheryl Karpen
Eleventh printing, August 2015

Homegrown in the USA

For more information or to locate a store near you, contact:
Gently Spoken
PO Box 245
Anoka, MN 55303

Toll-free 1-877-224-7886 or visit us online at
www.eatyourpeas.com

 30% post-consumer recycled paper